THE
LUTTRELL
VILLAGE

Also by Sheila Sancha
The Castle Story

THE
LUTTRELL
VILLAGE

Country Life in the Middle Ages

SHEILA SANCHA

Thomas Y. Crowell New York

Library of Congress Cataloging in Publication Data
Sancha, Sheila
   The Luttrell village.

   Summary: Traces a year in the Lincolnshire village of
Gerneham, from ploughing through sowing, harvesting, and
threshing, with illustrations of village life inspired
by the fourteenth-century Luttrell Psalter.
   1. England—Social life and customs—Medieval
period, 1066–1485—Juvenile literature.   2. Country life
—England—Juvenile literature.   3. Luttrell, Geoffrey,
Sir, d. 1345—Juvenile literature.   4. Gerneham
(Lincolnshire)—History—Juvenile literature.
[1. England—Social life and customs—Medieval period,
1066–1485.   2. Country life—England.   3. Villages.
4. Middle Ages]   I. Title.
DA185.S34 1982   306'.0942   82-45588
ISBN 0-690-04323-6
ISBN 0-690-04324-4 (lib. bdg.)

ACKNOWLEDGEMENTS

Firstly I would like to thank The British Library for
permission to use material from The Luttrell Psalter,
Additional MS 42130, and Janet Backhouse for her
advice. There are reproductions from the psalter in *The
Luttrell Psalter* published by the Trustees of the British
Museum in 1932, with the introduction and commentary
by Eric George Miller, M.A., D.Litt., F.S.A. and
although copies are rare, they can occasionally be
found in reference libraries.

   The easiest way of understanding the structure of
early timber buildings is to see reconstructions of them,
and I recommend visits to West Stow, Suffolk, and the
Weald and Downland Open Air Museum at Singleton,
near Chichester. I am indebted to the staff of The
Science Museum for solving several problems of
medieval technology; while invaluable information on
the early history of Irnham was supplied by David Roffe
of the South Lincolnshire Archaeological Unit.

   Expert advice and unflagging moral support came
from Susan Dickinson and Enid Fairhead of Collins,
editing the text and illustrations; and I was delighted
that my son-in-law, Doug Lear, did the lettering.

   Finally, I would like to thank Sir Simon and Lady
Benton Jones, who own the present Irnham estate, for
their enthusiasm and encouragement.

Sheila Sancha
LONDON 1982

This picture from the Luttrell Psalter shows Sir Geoffrey at dinner, served by his cup bearer. Sir Geoffrey's wife, Dame Agnes Sutton, sits on his right, whilst the two Dominican friars beyond, are probably his chaplain, Robert of Wilford, and his confessor, William of Foderingeye. The other figures are unidentified.

Irnham Village lies south of Lincoln on the edge of a limestone ridge that runs from Stamford to The Humber; it is to the east of Britain, inland from Boston and The Wash. In medieval times Lincolnshire was one of the most prosperous and densely populated counties in England, and Boston the third largest port. The village was probably founded by the Saxons, and was called Gerneham in the Domesday Survey of 1086.

Sometime between 1320 and 1340 Sir Geoffrey Luttrell, who owned the village, commissioned an unknown artist to make drawings of the villagers as they went about their work. Sir Geoffrey wanted to include pictures of himself and the familiar faces surrounding him in an elaborate prayer book that was being made for him. These books, called psalters, were quite common in medieval times. They contained psalms, prayers, and a calendar showing the seasons.

In this book I have attempted to put the people of the psalter back into their hills. Every scrap of available evidence was needed. I used map contours to make a relief model of the present Irnham estate, and set this alongside a tracing of a mid-eighteenth century map which supplied interesting field names. A high, rounded hill, once called the *Mill Field*, was obviously the site of the wind-mill in the psalter, while the adjacent *Great Land Field* is proof that the whole area was originally covered with the villagers' strips of land. Sheep now graze over another *Land Field*, where the pattern of medieval ridge and furrow is clearly visible. To avoid confusion, I have called this the *South Field*. There may have been only the two fields before 1340, but field names indicate some form of cultivation north of the village, and I have called this area the *New Field*.

Situated in a heavily-wooded limestone district, the lord's buildings would have been of either timber or stone. I have chosen the latter. The villagers would have lived in houses of timber, wattle and daub, or clay lump, and they may have carted stones from the fields for foundations and cobbles. The church is the only building to have survived from the fourteenth century although it was drastically altered a century later. It contains the tomb of Sir Geoffrey's grandfather, the brass to Andrew his eldest son, and an elaborate Easter Sepulchre that is hard to date, but certainly of the fourteenth century.

I have had to read many books and archaeological reports to reconstruct the village. But we can never know exactly where the individual people lived. Sir Geoffrey's hall probably stood next to the church on the site of the present Tudor hall. The psalter does not show many pictures of buildings, but a view of medieval Constantinople including inns and a church gave me the broomstick sign for the alehouse and the church weathercock. Irnham Hall has a fine park, and *Old Park Wood* stands opposite, just over the road. A *parker* is mentioned in Sir Geoffrey's will, and a deer park and private hunting ground would have existed in his time.

Sir Geoffrey Luttrell died in 1345 and is buried near the altar in Irnham church. The Luttrell Psalter lies under glass in The British Library's gallery in The British Museum in London.

BACK LANE

CROFT

TOFT

VILLAGE STREET

SMOKE-HOLE

SMOKE-HOLE

STRAW THATCH

COBBLES

OVEN

WALLS MADE OF BLOCKS OF UNBAKED CLAY

This is an ordinary house in the village of Gerneham on a cold winter's morning in the year 1328. The cobbled ground on which the house and sheds were built was called a **toft**, while the long stretch of land where vegetables grew in summer, and where sheep, goats, and pigs were kept in pens, was called a **croft**.

An entire family lived, ate and slept in the room in the middle of the house and smoke from the fire curled out of holes at the ends of the thatched roof. Ovens were either built outside in the toft or indoors behind a partition. The housewife would burn a bundle of wood inside the oven and, when the flames had died down, bake her bread on the ashes. The villager's two oxen were stabled beyond the passage. They were the pride of his life and he groomed them each day with a wisp of hay. After a breakfast of bread, cheese and thin ale, he and his son yoked them together, ready for the plough.

TOPS OF THE WOODEN COLLARS BEING PUSHED THROUGH HOLES IN THE YOKE

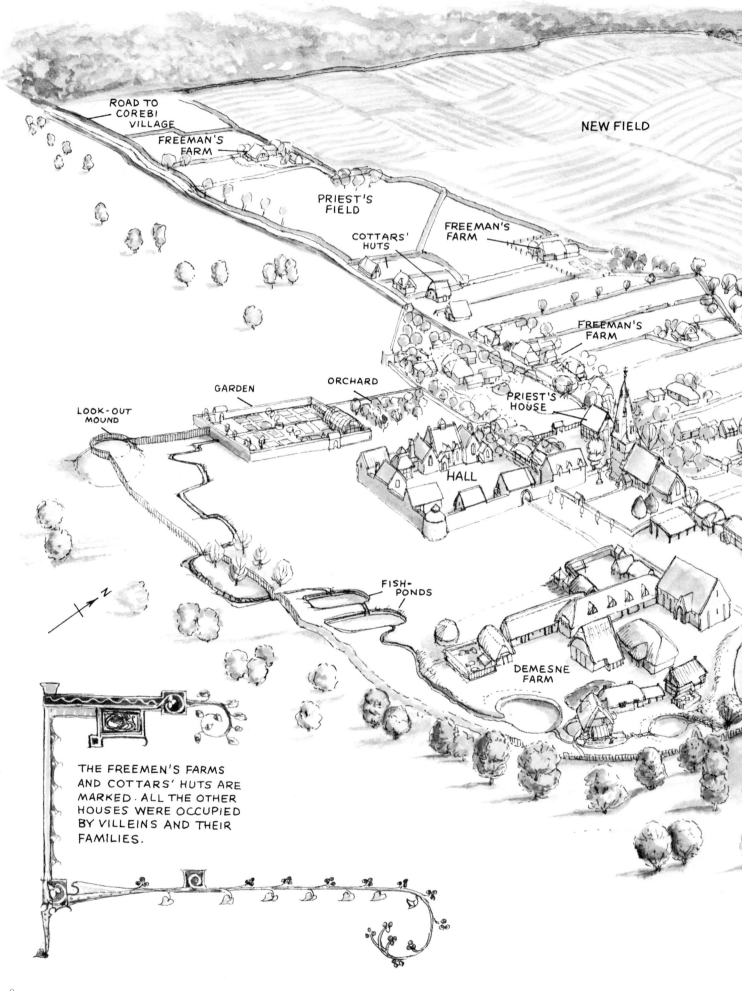

ROAD TO COREBI VILLAGE

FREEMAN'S FARM

NEW FIELD

PRIEST'S FIELD

COTTARS' HUTS

FREEMAN'S FARM

FREEMAN'S FARM

GARDEN

ORCHARD

PRIEST'S HOUSE

LOOK-OUT MOUND

HALL

FISH-PONDS

DEMESNE FARM

N

THE FREEMEN'S FARMS AND COTTARS' HUTS ARE MARKED. ALL THE OTHER HOUSES WERE OCCUPIED BY VILLEINS AND THEIR FAMILIES.

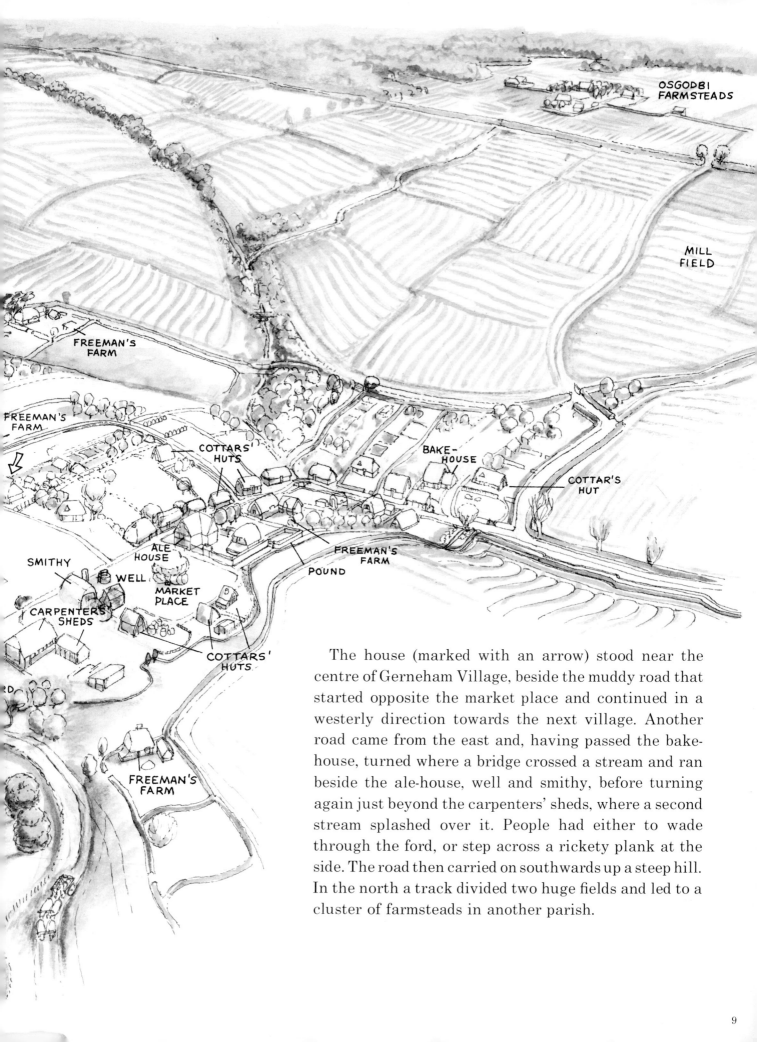

OSGODBI FARMSTEADS

MILL FIELD

FREEMAN'S FARM

FREEMAN'S FARM

COTTARS' HUTS

BAKE-HOUSE

COTTAR'S HUT

SMITHY

WELL

ALE HOUSE

MARKET PLACE

CARPENTERS SHEDS

COTTARS' HUTS

POUND

FREEMAN'S FARM

FREEMAN'S FARM

The house (marked with an arrow) stood near the centre of Gerneham Village, beside the muddy road that started opposite the market place and continued in a westerly direction towards the next village. Another road came from the east and, having passed the bake-house, turned where a bridge crossed a stream and ran beside the ale-house, well and smithy, before turning again just beyond the carpenters' sheds, where a second stream splashed over it. People had either to wade through the ford, or step across a rickety plank at the side. The road then carried on southwards up a steep hill. In the north a track divided two huge fields and led to a cluster of farmsteads in another parish.

While the men drove their oxen through the village to the field, the women and children carried jugs and wooden buckets to fetch the daily supply of water from the well. The village was said to have been founded by an Anglo-Saxon **thane** called Georna, and it was Georna's ham, or settlement. He had chosen this particular part of the forest because there were plenty of streams and underground springs, and the hills provided shelter from storms. Georna's men had sunk the well, and now it was the general meeting place for the women and children.

The men took the oxen up to the high land overlooking the village, the New Field, where wheat and a little rye had been harvested the previous autumn. It took teams of eight oxen to drag the ploughs up the narrow strips of heavy clay land. There were sixty-four oxen in the village; twenty-eight belonged to the lord, Sir Geoffrey, while the rest of the villagers, including the priest, had thirty-six oxen between them, which they lent to each other for the day's work. It took one day to plough one strip of land and each man had about thirty strips, sometimes less, sometimes more.

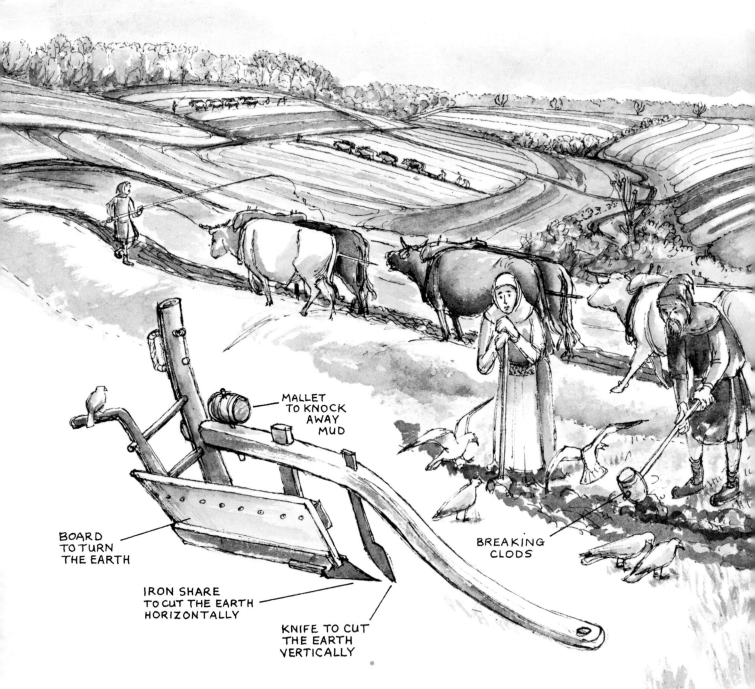

MALLET
TO KNOCK
AWAY
MUD

BOARD
TO TURN
THE EARTH

IRON SHARE
TO CUT THE EARTH
HORIZONTALLY

KNIFE TO CUT
THE EARTH
VERTICALLY

BREAKING
CLODS

The strips varied to fit the shape of the field, but on average they were 220 paces long and up to 22 paces wide. Because the ploughs travelled up and down, turning the soil towards the centre of the strips, the earth was gradually humped into ridges. Rainwater trickled down the slopes into furrows dividing one strip from another, and drained into a stream at the bottom of the field. The length of a strip was called a **furlong** (furrow-long), and the strips were arranged side by side in blocks, divided by tracks, banks or waste land. These blocks were also called **furlongs**.

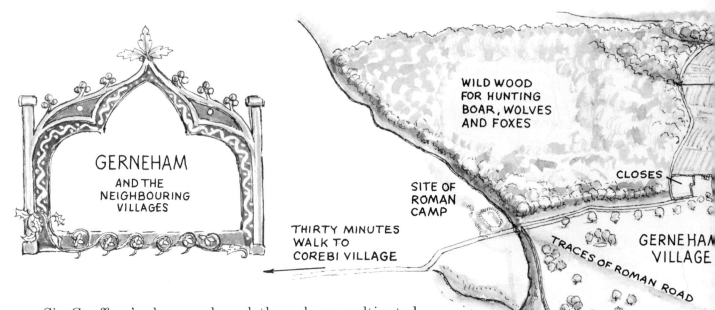

GERNEHAM
AND THE
NEIGHBOURING
VILLAGES

WILD WOOD
FOR HUNTING
BOAR, WOLVES
AND FOXES

CLOSES

SITE OF
ROMAN
CAMP

TRACES OF ROMAN ROAD

GERNEHAM
VILLAGE

THIRTY MINUTES
WALK TO
COREBI VILLAGE

RABBIT
WARREN

TIMBER
WOOD

ONE HOUR'S
WALK TO
SWINEHAMSTED
VILLAGE

TWO HOUR'S
WALK TO
CASTLE
BITHAM

Sir Geoffrey's deer park and three huge cultivated fields surrounded Gerneham Village. Autumn-sown wheat and rye was already coming up in the Mill Field, where the mill sails turned at the top of the hill. Sheep cropped the dry stalks of last autumn's bean, oat and barley harvest in the South Field on the opposite side of the road. No crops would be lifted from these strips this year, the field would be left **fallow** for the soil to become fertile again. Manure from the precious dung heaps in the crofts and marl (a mixture of lime and clay) would be spread over the strips and they would not be ploughed until the spring. They would be ploughed or "stirred" a couple of times after that to destroy weeds, before being sown with wheat and rye in the autumn.

In early times there had been only two fields: one for crops and one to be left fallow, but it was discovered that fields could be harvested two years in succession and still yield good crops, if left fallow every third year. Therefore a third field was needed. At this particular season the men were busy ploughing the wheat stubble in the New Field which their grandfathers had cleared on the hillside overlooking the village.

Closes were the small pockets of hedged or fenced land owned either by Sir Geoffrey or by some of the more prosperous villagers. Although crops were occasionally grown in closes, they were mostly used as grazing land for horses, bulls, cows and other animals that had to be kept away from the common herd.

14

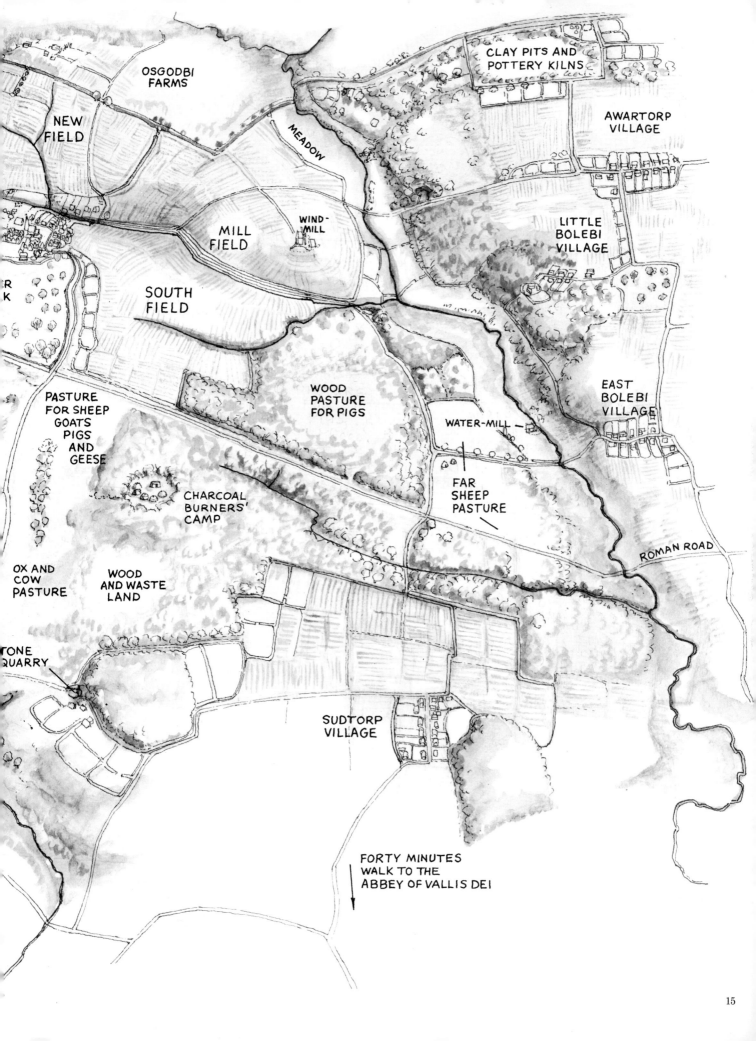

CLAY PITS AND POTTERY KILNS

OSGODBI FARMS

AWARTORP VILLAGE

NEW FIELD

MEADOW

LITTLE BOLEBI VILLAGE

MILL FIELD

WIND-MILL

R K

SOUTH FIELD

EAST BOLEBI VILLAGE

PASTURE FOR SHEEP GOATS PIGS AND GEESE

WOOD PASTURE FOR PIGS

WATER-MILL

FAR SHEEP PASTURE

CHARCOAL BURNERS' CAMP

ROMAN ROAD

OX AND COW PASTURE

WOOD AND WASTE LAND

TONE QUARRY

SUDTORP VILLAGE

FORTY MINUTES WALK TO THE ABBEY OF VALLIS DEI

When there was a suspicion of warmth in the blustery wind, it was time to sow barley in the New Field. The best sheaves had been carefully put aside last autumn, after the South Field had been harvested, and now they had been threshed and the seed carted out to the field.

Pigeons from Sir Geoffrey's and the priest's dovecotes followed the carts, while rooks and crows rose cawing from the nearby wood, swooped down and fought over the grain as soon as it was out of the sacks. Some boys did their best to hit the crows with sling-stones, but they were forbidden to kill pigeons because they belonged to their lord and to the church. One man scattered the seed, while another followed with a horse-drawn harrow, covering the seed as quickly as possible. It was always a battle with the birds.

DIRECTION OF WIND

WIDOW BRINGING BARLEY

MILLER TURNING THE MILL TO FACE THE WIND

MILL HOUSE

MILL LAD PULLING THE LINEN AND HEMP SAILS OVER THEIR WOODEN FRAMES

Some of last year's barley was malted and used by the ale-wife at the inn for brewing her ale, but the rest was crushed between mill-stones and ground to flour. The best bread was made of wheat, but the villagers also made barley or rye-bread and when their sacks were getting empty at the hungry time of the year – before the next harvest – they put beans into the dough. Sir Geoffrey owned the mills, and the millers paid him a rent and had the monopoly of the business. Villagers were not allowed to grind corn on little hand-mills at home, but had to carry their sacks to the miller, who took a measure of corn in return for the grinding. The water-mill had been down by the stream ever since Saxon times (although frequently rebuilt), but wind-mills were a new invention and had been in general use only for the past hundred years.

WITH A CHANGE OF WIND THE TAIL POLE IS PUSHED ROUND AND THE MILL TURNS WHERE THE TOP OF THE POST FITS INTO A SOCKET IN THE BEAM

TAIL POLE

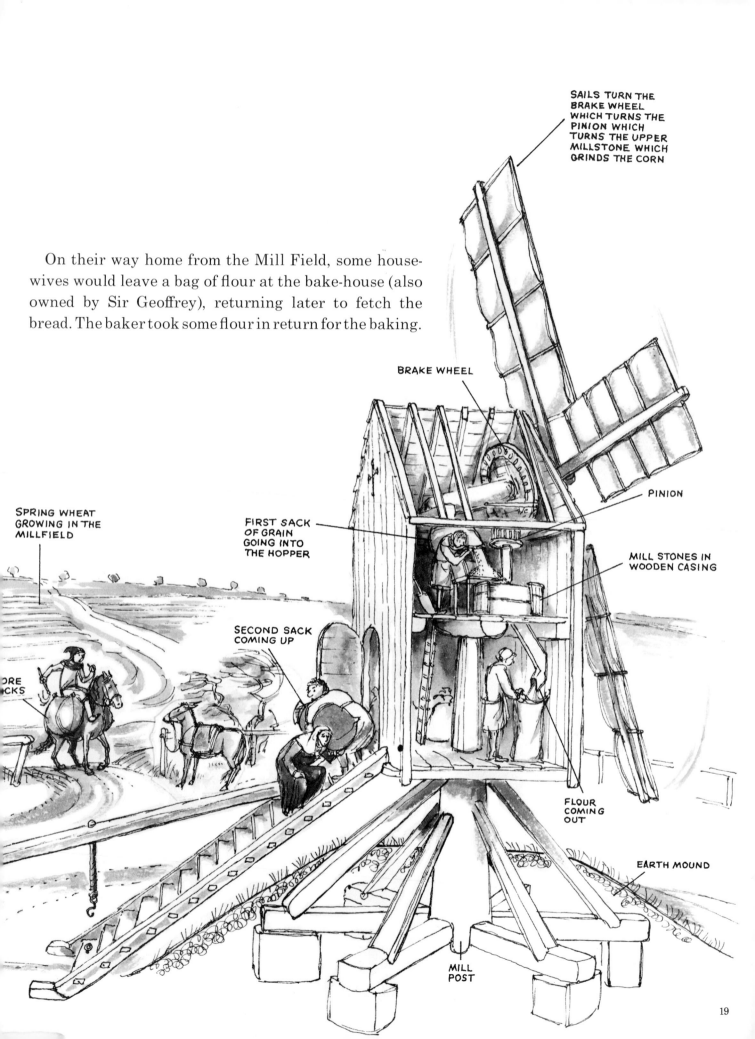

On their way home from the Mill Field, some house-wives would leave a bag of flour at the bake-house (also owned by Sir Geoffrey), returning later to fetch the bread. The baker took some flour in return for the baking.

SAILS TURN THE BRAKE WHEEL WHICH TURNS THE PINION WHICH TURNS THE UPPER MILLSTONE WHICH GRINDS THE CORN

BRAKE WHEEL

PINION

SPRING WHEAT GROWING IN THE MILLFIELD

FIRST SACK OF GRAIN GOING INTO THE HOPPER

MILL STONES IN WOODEN CASING

SECOND SACK COMING UP

ORE CKS

FLOUR COMING OUT

EARTH MOUND

MILL POST

19

Although the villagers worked together in the fields they were by no means equal. Some were **freemen**: small-time farmers who owned or rented their houses and land. They even rode horses and could come and go as they pleased. Others were **villeins** who had no freedom at all. Everything they had belonged to Sir Geoffrey, including their houses, land, animals, and even their wives and children. They not only had to grow their own food, but were obliged to spend two or three days a week labouring on Sir Geoffrey's strips out in the fields. Other villagers were poor **cottars** who often had no strips at all, only the land round their cottages. They worked for wages or followed other trades, such as basket-weaving or bee-keeping.

Each year the villagers elected a **reeve** to defend their rights at the manor court and to organize their work. There was also a **hayward** to see that the ditches were kept clear, and the hedges in good repair. In a larger village, Sir Geoffrey would have employed a **pinder** to round up stray animals and lock them in the **pound** until the owners paid a fine to collect them; but as it was, the hayward undertook the unpopular job.

REEVE

HAYWARD

HAYWARD'S LAD

POUND

FREEMEN (COMPLAINING ABOUT THE WEATHER)

VILLEINS (LISTENING TO THEIR REEVE)

WATER CARRIER

MOLE-CATCHER

BEE-KEEPER

COTTARS

BEGGARS

Spring came. The cuckoos and swallows arrived. The grass started to grow, and the older children drove their parents' sheep and goats past the deer park and up to the common land on the high pasture beyond the Roman road. Behind the high palisade, the fallow deer had bitten off every oak shoot within reach. Only mature trees could survive unprotected in a deer park, and the newly-planted saplings were ringed round with stout posts and rails.

Sir Geoffrey's shepherds drove his flocks up the hill and turned left along the Roman road towards the far pasture by the meadows. Many long-legged horned sheep looked like goats, and Sir Geoffrey kept a special breed (imported by the Vikings) which had two horns sticking out in front and two more curving behind. The flocks followed leading rams that were fitted with bells. Shepherds had only to listen to discover their whereabouts.

One evening, as the shepherds were bringing their flocks home to be milked, they heard the beat of horses' hooves on the worn stones of the Roman road. Sir Geoffrey and Dame Agnes, his wife, were coming to spend a few weeks at Gerneham. It was a fine cavalcade. Sir Geoffrey always travelled with a household of about a hundred people: his children, friends, chaplains, squires, waiting women, servants and pages. Dame Agnes, exhausted by travelling, sat in a carriage, but everyone else rode splendid horses (quite a different breed from the freemen's horses). The three squires riding in front halted at the crest of the hill and blew loud trumpet blasts to announce their arrival.

GARDEN

ORCHARD

HALL

DOG KENNELS

HAWKS' MEWS

STEWARD'S CHAMBER OVER STORE ROOMS

KITCHEN

BREW-HOUSE

BAKE-HOUSE

MALTING-HOUSE

DOVE-COTE

ARMOURY

GATE-HOUSE

FISH PONDS

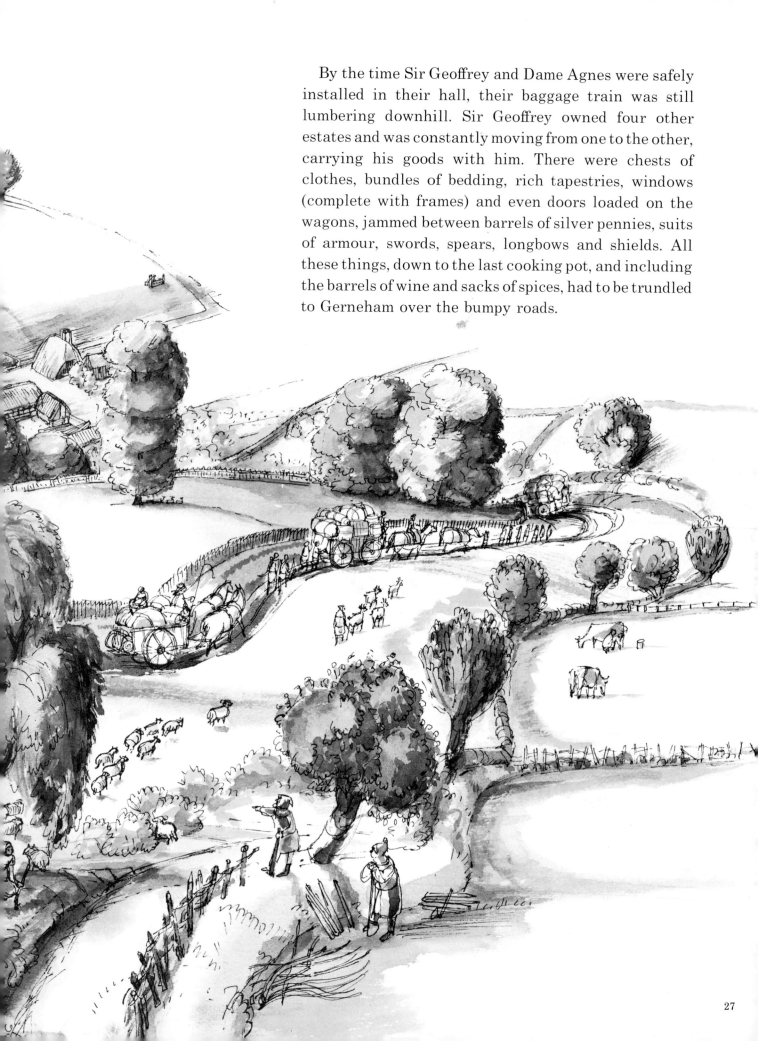

By the time Sir Geoffrey and Dame Agnes were safely installed in their hall, their baggage train was still lumbering downhill. Sir Geoffrey owned four other estates and was constantly moving from one to the other, carrying his goods with him. There were chests of clothes, bundles of bedding, rich tapestries, windows (complete with frames) and even doors loaded on the wagons, jammed between barrels of silver pennies, suits of armour, swords, spears, longbows and shields. All these things, down to the last cooking pot, and including the barrels of wine and sacks of spices, had to be trundled to Gerneham over the bumpy roads.

BREW-
HOUSE

KITCHEN

STEWARD

BAILIFF

A household of over a hundred persons consumed an immense amount of food. Sir Geoffrey would stay at Gerneham until the fish-ponds, deer park, rabbit warren and pigeon-cote were thinning out, and the barns were empty, before leaving for another estate. The main meal was about mid-day and the menu was mostly meat. Animals had been slaughtered in readiness by order of the **steward**, the man in charge of the Gerneham estate when Sir Geoffrey was away. The steward would tell the **bailiff** what was needed and the bailiff saw the orders were carried out. Most of the meat was roasted outside, and only more specialised cooking was done under the high kitchen roof. Bread was baked in a bake-house and ale brewed in a brew-house.

CHAMBER
WITH PANTRY
FOR BREAD
BELOW

KITCHEN

BUTTERY
FOR WINE

STAIRS
TO CHAPLAIN'S
ROOM

There was not much accommodation for so many people in a hall and two chambers. Sir Geoffrey and Dame Agnes had four children. The eldest son was already married and he and his wife used the chamber over the buttery and pantry, sharing it with friends and other members of the family. Important guests slept in

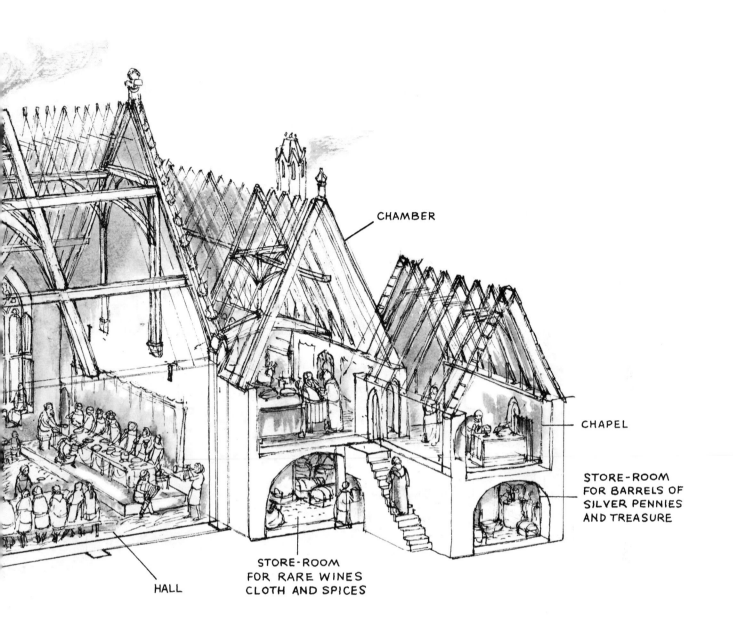

CHAMBER

CHAPEL

STORE-ROOM
FOR BARRELS OF
SILVER PENNIES
AND TREASURE

STORE-ROOM
FOR RARE WINES
CLOTH AND SPICES

HALL

make-shift beds in Sir Geoffrey's chamber at the other end of the hall, their squires lying by the doorways or curled up in corners of the room. Everyone else threw down palliasses in the barns, or slept on the rushes by the hall fire, or the cobbles of the store-rooms, wherever they could find a space. When the household packed up and left, the rushes would be swept away and the whole building given a thorough cleaning. The steward and bailiff acted as caretakers.

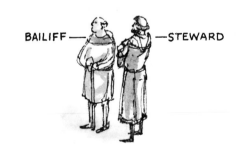

BAILIFF

STEWARD

Private conversations were impossible in such crowded places and when they had something serious to discuss, Sir Geoffrey and Dame Agnes would walk together through the closely-planted orchard or talk in the arbour of their pleasure garden, hidden by climbing roses and vines. Round three sides of the arbour there was a bank, planted with grass and herbs, where people could sit. The garden had stone walls, a well, and a stream running through it. A gardener and his boy looked after the rectangular flower beds, bright with roses, lilies, daisies and sweet-smelling herbs.

Vegetables were more important than flowers in cottage gardens. A villein's wife spent most of the summer digging, weeding and growing plants for the pot. Rich people could eat meat, but the poor had to make do on cabbages, onions, beans and peas, although there was usually a bit of salt bacon left over from the pig that had been killed before Christmas. There were chickens and eggs, if the hens were laying. Most villagers grew flax to be woven into linen sheets and shirts, and hemp for sacks and rope. All these crops had to be weeded.

CHEESE MOULD

BUTTER CHURN

As well as gardening, the villeins' wives had to milk their sheep and goats. Occasionally, the cream was skimmed off the milk and churned to butter, but mostly the milk was put aside with a little rennet (liquid from a calf's stomach) and left to divide into curds and whey. The curds (solids) slowly turned to cheese as the whey (water) dripped through a strainer. Then the cheese was put in a cheese mould under a stone to press out the rest of the whey. Children drank the whey with their bread and cheese, and so nothing was wasted.

DISTAFF

SPINDLE

Sheep were shorn about mid-summer. After the thick fleeces had been washed in the stream, the wool was combed between spiked boards to pull every strand in the same direction. This was called carding. The carded wool was then tied to the end of a distaff and the village women spent every spare moment twirling their spindles, twisting the wool into spun yarn. Spinning wheels were rare. The yarn was woven into lengths which were finally cut and stitched into tunics, hoods, cloaks and gowns to keep the family warm in the coming winter.

No one was allowed to be idle. Girls lent a hand in the meadow by the water-mill where the hay was being mown, while their mothers carried down baskets of bread, cheese, and salt fish for the mid-day meal in a returning cart. There were jugs of ale for the men and whey for the children. The miller sold eels from traps he had set in the stream.

The steward gave orders to the reeve, who was in charge of the mowing. At the sight of the food-cart, the hayward blew his horn as a signal for everyone to knock off work. The mown hay was dried in haycocks before being forked on to the carts and each villein took home his **dole**, or share of the hay. When the haymaking was over, the oxen were allowed to graze in the meadows.

The lord's share of the hay was carted over the hills and up the slope to the **demesne** farm. The **manor** referred to the whole of the Gerneham territory, inclusive of buildings; but the demesne (to rhyme with "rain") referred only to the land directly under Sir Geoffrey's control. It did not include the villeins' lands, or the small holdings rented or owned by the freemen.

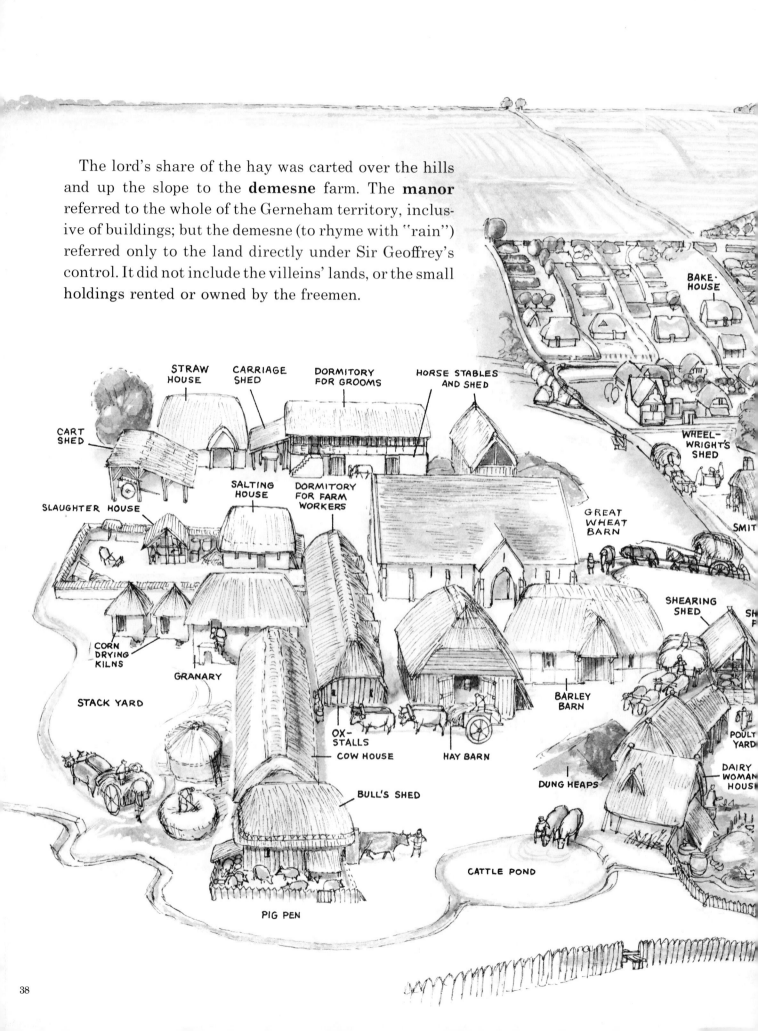

BAKE-HOUSE

WHEEL-WRIGHT'S SHED

STRAW HOUSE

CARRIAGE SHED

DORMITORY FOR GROOMS

HORSE STABLES AND SHED

CART SHED

SALTING HOUSE

DORMITORY FOR FARM WORKERS

GREAT WHEAT BARN

SMIT

SLAUGHTER HOUSE

CORN DRYING KILNS

GRANARY

STACK YARD

SHEARING SHED

SH

OX-STALLS

COW HOUSE

HAY BARN

BARLEY BARN

POULT YARD

BULL'S SHED

DUNG HEAPS

DAIRY WOMAN HOUS

PIG PEN

CATTLE POND

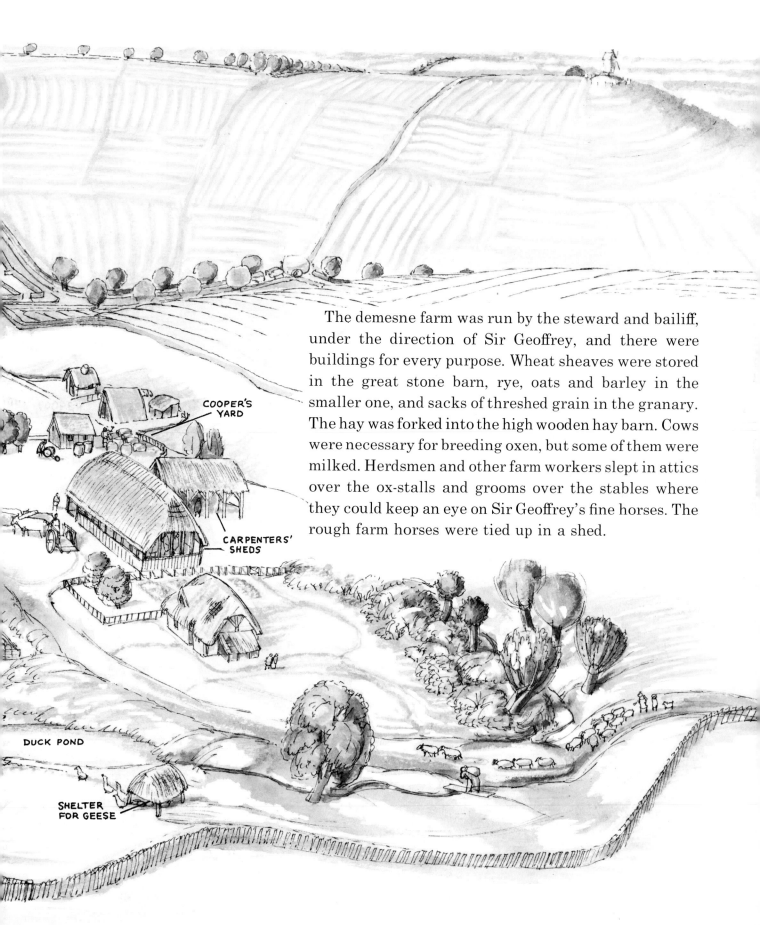

COOPER'S YARD

CARPENTERS' SHEDS

DUCK POND

SHELTER FOR GEESE

The demesne farm was run by the steward and bailiff, under the direction of Sir Geoffrey, and there were buildings for every purpose. Wheat sheaves were stored in the great stone barn, rye, oats and barley in the smaller one, and sacks of threshed grain in the granary. The hay was forked into the high wooden hay barn. Cows were necessary for breeding oxen, but some of them were milked. Herdsmen and other farm workers slept in attics over the ox-stalls and grooms over the stables where they could keep an eye on Sir Geoffrey's fine horses. The rough farm horses were tied up in a shed.

The widowed poultry-woman lived in the yard next to the sheep-pen, surrounded by hens, ducks, geese and peacocks. Her daughters milked the lord's sheep each morning before the shepherds took them out to pasture, and again when they returned at night. Some flocks were kept out all night on the far hills now that it was high summer, and milked by the shepherds. The poultry-woman turned the milk to butter and cheeses for the people up at the hall, and also supplied plucked poultry and eggs. She stock-piled the cheeses, storing them on the dairy shelves, for use in the winter.

Gerneham Village had a weekly market, and a mid-summer fair which lasted several days. People flocked to the fair from miles around to buy up surplus produce, and this was about the only time the villeins handled real money. They used it to buy knives, shears, needles,

cooking pots and pans, and other necessities that could not be made at home, from the merchants who arrived in carts, or leading strings of packhorses. Only freemen's wives could afford silk ribbons, spices, and good quality cloth. The ale-wife did a roaring trade at the inn.

43

Summer turned to autumn and it was time for the wheat and rye harvest. Every able-bodied soul in the village had to work in the Mill Field while the sun still shone. If it rained, the grain would go mouldy, and that would mean a hungry winter ahead. The crops grew taller than they do now. The wheat was cut about half way up the stalks, bound into sheaves, and set on end to dry. After the last sheaf had been safely carted away, the cottars' wives and other poor folk searched the field for any stray ears of grain (this was called gleaning). Later the remaining short stalks were scythed and used as bedding straw for cattle. Afterwards sheep and oxen roamed over the empty field to graze. The manure was good for the land.

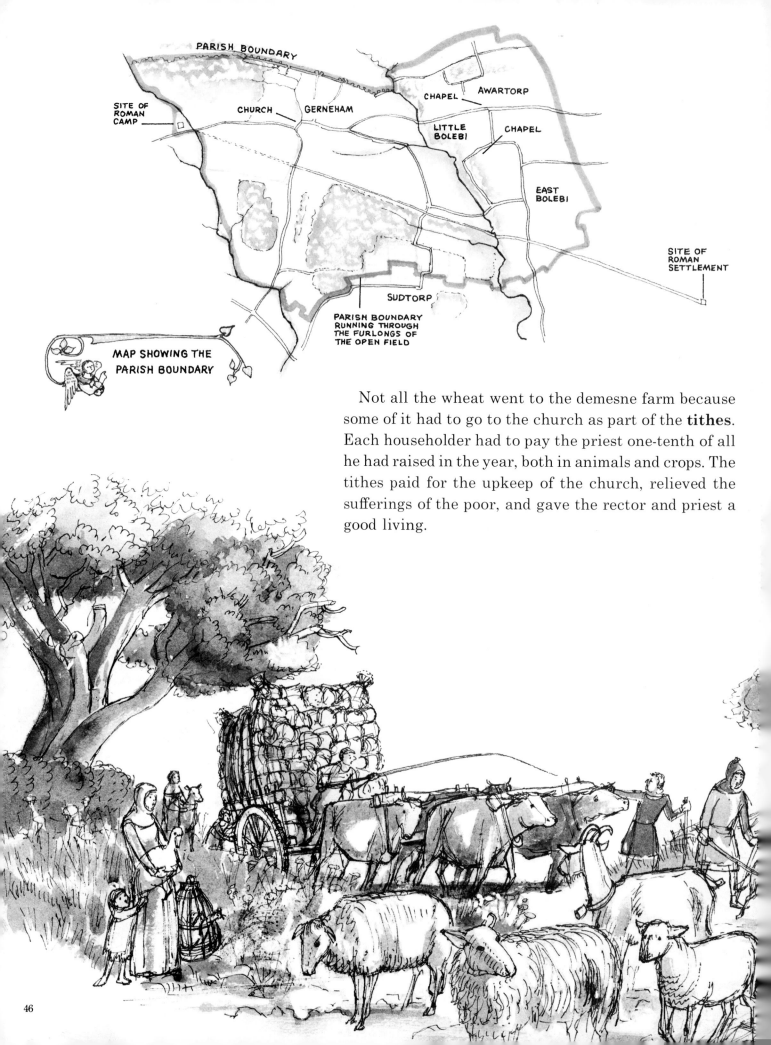

PARISH BOUNDARY

SITE OF
ROMAN
CAMP

CHURCH   GERNEHAM

CHAPEL   AWARTORP

LITTLE
BOLEBI

CHAPEL

EAST
BOLEBI

SITE OF
ROMAN
SETTLEMENT

SUDTORP

PARISH BOUNDARY
RUNNING THROUGH
THE FURLONGS OF
THE OPEN FIELD

MAP SHOWING THE
PARISH BOUNDARY

Not all the wheat went to the demesne farm because some of it had to go to the church as part of the **tithes**. Each householder had to pay the priest one-tenth of all he had raised in the year, both in animals and crops. The tithes paid for the upkeep of the church, relieved the sufferings of the poor, and gave the rector and priest a good living.

Sir Geoffrey's brother was **rector** of Gerneham, but he was always away, saying Masses in more important churches. Most of the proceeds of the tithes were passed on to him: only about one third of the tithes were kept by the priest who actually held the services. The priest, who had a deacon to help him, was an ordinary villager, without much book-learning, but he understood farming. When the tithes came in, he put the grain in his barn and the animals in pens, or in the large field owned by the church. Sometimes he grazed calves in the churchyard and stored sacks of grain in the church. He also received produce from the three other villages of the **parish**. Animals and grain could be converted to money on market days, or at the fair.

LATE
THIRTEENTH
CENTURY
SPIRE

LATE
TWELFTH
CENTURY
TOWER

BELLS
CALLING
PEOPLE
TO
MASS

THIRTEENTH CENTURY NAVE

PRIEST

DEACON

Village life centred round the church. Each Sunday the inhabitants of all three villages crowded into the **nave** to hear Mass while their priest pulled a fine embroidered vestment over his grubby cassock and said prayers from the **chancel**. The chancel was sacred to God, while the nave was treated as a village hall, used for meetings and even for games. Children were taught lessons in the church porch, and occasionally there was dancing in the churchyard.

Once there had been a wooden church, but it had been demolished sometime before 1180 when the villagers built a square bell tower with a massive round arch out of local stone. The church was not finished until the late thirteenth century when building methods had improved and pointed arches come into fashion. Gerneham was a well-to-do village and the fine carved windows with their coloured glass had been paid for by the bumper harvests of the past fifty years. An artist had painted pictures all over the plastered walls.

PRIEST ROBED FOR MASS

LATE THIRTEENTH CENTURY CHANCEL

THE SOUTH WALL AND PARTS OF THE ROOF HAVE BEEN REMOVED TO SHOW THE INTERIOR OF THE CHURCH

SIR GEOFFREY'S GRANDFATHER LIES IN THE TOMB. HE DIED IN 1270

PRIESTS' SEATS

TOMB

PATRON SAINT

After the last of the bean, oat and barley harvest had been carried from the New Field, the villagers took their tools to the smith to be sharpened and mended. The smiths and carpenters had their workshops alongside each other, with the wheelwright and cooper adjoining, making cart-wheels and barrels. The smiths made plough-shares, axes, scythes and other tools, while the carpenters supplied the handles and made the wooden parts of the carts, ploughs and harrows. Freemen brought their horses to be shod at the smithy, and even some oxen were fitted with iron shoes on their cloven hooves.

The carpenters also made houses. Wooden houses never lasted long and when someone needed a new house, trees were felled on the wasteland, up by the cow pasture, and carted down to the carpenters' sheds. Roughly-squared oak trunks made posts and beams for the timber framework and slender ash poles were used for the roof. Slats of wood were slid into grooves between the posts and beams and a wattlework of willow or hazel wands woven round them. Finally a mixture of clay, chopped straw, ox-hair and dung was daubed on both sides of the wattlework until the **wattle and daub** wall was solid, ready to be plastered. Reeds from the stream, or straw, made the thatch, but sometimes houses were roofed with turf or bundles of brushwood. Wattlework was also used for fences.

TREE TRUNKS

SPLIT
ASH
POLE

WILLOW
WANDS

HAZEL
POSTS

Autumn was the season for the fallow South Field to be sown with wheat and a small quantity of rye, for the coming year. A hedge marked the boundary of the field and it was the hayward's job to keep it repaired.

HAZEL BUSHES

OSIERS FOR BASKETWORK

The special timber, to be used on Sir Geoffrey's buildings, came from the Timber Wood, alongside the common pasture land. There was a high bank, a wide ditch, and a hedge to keep the animals out of the wood. Tall straight oaks were needed for the posts and beams of houses and barns. The wind-mill post had come from this wood. Ash and alder trees were coppiced to make the long roofing poles. **Coppicing** was done by felling trees and letting them shoot from the base, while **pollarding** was done by cutting them at a higher level and letting them shoot out of reach of goats and the other animals that would eat the young leaves. Trees were pollarded in places were there were loose animals about.

Along the north side of the Roman road was another stretch of woodland, full of ancient oaks and beech trees. Each frosty morning in late autumn the swineherds went the rounds of the cottages collecting the villagers' pigs and, together with Sir Geoffrey's pig herd from the demesne farm, they drove them to the wood to feed on the acorns and beech-mast that fell from the trees.

This open grassy wood was kept almost entirely for pig-pasture, or **pannage**. Throughout the summer, the pigs had rooted about for food on the high waste lands up by the cow-pasture.

Autumn was a time of plenty, especially on a freeman's farm, and the housewives had to prepare for the hard winter ahead. Although there was hay and straw heaped up in the crofts, there were no proper foodstuffs for the animals, and most of them had to be killed off, only the best being kept until spring. Pork was the main meat. When a pig was killed, the meat was soaked in salt water before being hung in the smoke over the hearth. Sea-salt came to the village from salt-pans on the coast, about a day's journey away.

Winter came with a flurry of snow, and when the weather was too bad for outside work, the villagers began threshing their grain. The freemen did their threshing in their own small barns, but the villeins had stored their wheat sheaves in the great barn on the demesne farm. The reeve had notched on his **tally sticks** the exact number of sheaves each man had grown on his strips of land, and allotted the sacks of grain accordingly. The barn doors were built opposite each other, and the wind rushed through and blew away the husks as the villeins' wives tossed the grain with round winnowing fans. The villeins put their grain into sacks and carried it home, while Sir Geoffrey's grain was stored in his granary. The remaining straw went to the stables as bedding for horses and oxen.

All tools were put away when Christmas came round and for twelve whole days the inhabitants of Gerneham gave themselves up to the business of eating, drinking, playing games, and dancing to boisterous music. The first Sunday after Twelfth Night marked the end of the festivities and a plough was taken to the church to receive the priest's blessing. The next day the village lads dragged the plough round all the houses, singing and cracking whips to drive away evil spirits. It was Plough Monday, and the year's work was about to begin all over again.

GLOSSARY

Bailiff 28–9 The official who made sure the orders of his lord, or steward, were carried out. He checked how many days the villeins worked on the lord's land, and supervised the herdsmen tending the animals on the demesne farm. He summoned villagers to the manor courts, and punished criminals.

Chancel 48–9 The eastern end of a church, held sacred and only to be used by the priest and the choir.

Close 14–5 A piece of land enclosed by a hedge, fence etc. In fact, a small field.

Coppicing 54–5 Chopping down trees at ground level and allowing new shoots to sprout from the stump. The shoots were cut once they had grown to a suitable length to be used for roofing poles, fencing, and other purposes. A coppice was a small wood where this had been done.

Cottar 20–1 One of the poorest of the villagers, who had a cottage and croft, but no strips to cultivate out in the fields. Also called a *bordar* (from *bordarius*, which is medieval Latin for a hut).

Croft 6–7 A useful stretch of fenced land adjoining a villager's house, where animals, poultry and bees were kept, and where crops, vegetables, flax, herbs and trees were grown.

Demesne 38–9 The land belonging to a lord that was cultivated entirely for his own use, and not tenanted out, or let to anyone else. Buildings for the lord's animals and crops were grouped together on the *demesne* farm.

Dole 36–7 When meadowland, animal fodder, goods etc were being divided among the villagers, each person's share was called a *dole*. It usually indicated a small amount.

Fallow 14–5 Ground that was ploughed, but not sown with any seed. If crops were grown year after year in the same place, all the nourishment was taken out of the soil, resulting in increasingly poor harvests. Soil was enriched with manure, and marl (lime and clay) and broken up by a winter's frost. It was common practice for land to be left fallow every two or three years.

Freeman 20–1 A man who was free to travel and not compelled to spend all his life in the village, like the villeins. He did not have to work on the lord's land, but owed "suite and service", which entailed following the lord to war, riding messages (many freemen owned horses), paying fees and fines, and attending the manor court. A freeman either owned his own house and land, or was a tenant paying rent.

Furlong 12–3 A land measurement of about 220 yards, (about 200 metres) being the length of an average furrow. Where strips were ploughed alongside each other in a block, measuring roughly a furlong each way, this block was also called a furlong.

Ham 10–11 Anglo-Saxon word for a homestead or village.

Hayward 20–1 The man who supervised the upkeep of hedges and ditches and who also acted as pinder if it was a small village.

Manor 38–9 The lord's hall, the out-buildings, and all the land belonging to him, including the pockets of land tenanted out to freemen and the villagers' strips in the fields. Arguments were settled, and wrong-doers tried in the *manor court* with the lord, or the steward, acting as judge. These courts were held in the lord's hall, in the church nave, or – weather permitting – under a convenient tree.

Marl 14–5 A mixture of lime and clay spread over the land to improve the soil.

Nave 48–9 The part of a church used by the congregation. There were no pews in early medieval times and people either stood, sat on the floor, or leaned against walls and pillars.

Pannage 56–7 The feeding of swine in the autumn in a wood where beech-mast and acorns lay on the ground. Swine being the old name for pig, pannage was also called pig-pasture.

Parish 46–7 An area of land enclosing one, or several, villages, where the priest could look after the spiritual welfare of the inhabitants. In return, the parishioners had to pay tithes. Parish boundaries had been fixed well before the Norman Conquest by the church authorities.

Pinder 20–1 The man employed by the lord to catch stray animals and keep them in the village pound, or pinfold. The owners paid a fine to collect them. In a small village the hayward often acted as Pinder.

Pollarding 54–5 Similar to coppicing, but instead of cutting the trees at ground level, lopping the trunks at a sufficient height to allow them to sprout above the heads of animals that might eat the young shoots. For this reason trees were pollarded on roadsides or near the common pastures.

Pound 20–1 A walled or fenced yard where animals were detained or *impounded*.

Rector 46–7 A priest who had charge of churches and parishes receiving the tithes and other dues from his parishioners. Where a rector had many parishes and could not to take all the services, he would install vicars to do the work for him – the vicars receiving some of the tithes.

Reeve 20–1 In Saxon times the reeve was an important man, organizing the village work and taking orders only from the thane. But after the Norman Conquest the Saxon reeves had to obey the Norman stewards and their authority was diminished. They were then elected by the villagers to supervise their work and defend their interests at the manor courts.

Steward 28–9 The lord's deputy, when the lord was away. He was given great authority, organizing work, seeing to the upkeep of buildings, and sitting in judgement at the manor court.

Tally-sticks 60–1 Sticks used for reckoning accounts. The required number of lines were scratched across a small rectangular piece of wood which was then split down the middle, and each party to an agreement kept one of the halves (like an invoice).

Thane 10–11 An Anglo-Saxon nobleman and landowner.

Tithes 46–7 One-tenth of the produce of every family in the parish had to be paid to the church. *Great tithes* were the main crops, such as grain, hay, wood and fruit, while the *small tithes* were the little things that were often hand-made, such as baskets and shoes, or a mixture of objects.

Toft 6–7 The plot of land on which a villager built his hut or house. Once the house was up and the surrounding ground cobbled, the toft looked much the same as a back yard.

Villeins 20–1 Villagers who belonged to their lord and never allowed to leave the village unless they were sold to somebody else. They had no rights in law. In exchange for the use of their cottages and land, they had to work two or three days a week on the lord's land. They were also called bondsmen, and sometimes called serfs but this word, derived from the Latin *servus*, really describes a person who was a complete slave.

Wattle and Daub 52–3 The daub was a building material of clay, straw, hair, etc, which was plastered on both sides of the wattle – thin strips of wood wound in and out of wooden stakes. This hurdle-work was fitted into the main timber framework of a house.

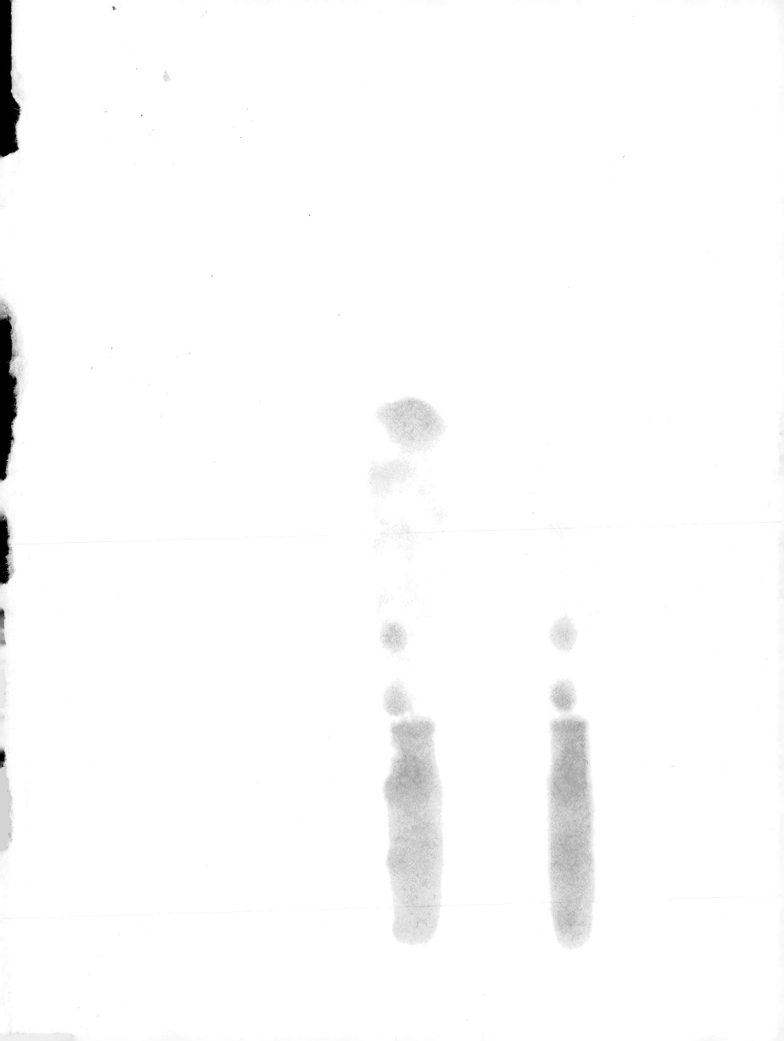